BAOBAB PUBLISHING

PLANTING SEEDS OF CHARACTER, WISDOM, UNITY, AND LOVE

Text Copyright © 2015
by Schertevear Q. Watkins and Susieann Beavers Harris
Address all inquiries to:
Baobab Books
Email: bbfbooks@gmail.com
ISBN-13:
978-1-947045-13-2 (Baobab Publishing)

Author's Bio

Schertevear Watkins is a former educator and divorced mother of two. Her love for teaching is her inspiration for writing Children's Literature. Schertevear's goal is to bring positive influences into the lives of as many children as possible through her characters. Schertevear writes books that promote learning, character development, social skills, family and more.

Author's Bio

Susieann Beavers-Harris is a former Pre-kindergarten transition coach and has volunteered in Pre-K classrooms. In the classroom, she saw the area's most challenging for early learners.
Knowing that there are many children that need the extra preparation for elementary school, Susieann was inspired to contribute to this learning series.

LOOK OUT FOR THESE OTHER TITLES FROM

BLOOMING READERS

on

and baobabpublishing.com

Basic Sight Word Book

Basic Sight Word: People, Places and Things Book

Basic Sight Word: Action Word Book

Basic Sight Word: Look, Taste. Feel, Smell and Sound Book

Basic Sight Word: Pronoun Book

Basic Sight Word: Careers Book

THIS BOOK BELONGS TO

_____

Describing Words

LOOK, TASTE, FEEL, SMELL AND SOUND

My name is Shana and this is my *Describing Word Book*. Describing words are called adjectives. Adjectives help describe how people places and things around you look, taste, feel, smell and sound. Let me describe some people places and things around me.

Shana

The purpose of learning these sight words is for Early Readers to learn how to put words together to form sentences.

Cousin Chad feels *sick* so he went to bed early.

My big sister Angela wore a *lovely*
new dress to her prom.

My uncle has a *big* white house across town.

The neighbor's *dirty, smelly* dog needs a bath.

My friend Kayley is *nice*
because she always shares.

Corey wore a hat and gloves today
because it was *cold*.

Emma was cute and chubby when she was a baby.

My aunt Mini was *happy* when her garden bloomed.

Tyson was *surprised* when Daddy bought him a car.

The icing on Troy's birthday cake
was too *sweet*.

I think it is *mean* when the kids at school call Christie *ugly* because she is a troll.

My uncle Bruce can run very *fast*.

Cara's grandma is *old*,
but Meagan's grandma is not.

My brother Tray is *slim* and *shy*.

Eboni was *sad*
when her mom brought her to school.

Steve was *angry* with Marcus for snatching his toy.

The plates are *clean* because my mom washed dishes.

Dad will be late coming home because traffic is *slow*.

Lucy is *short* and her grandpa is *tall*.

When it gets *hot* outside my friend Nikki swims in her pool.

Goldilocks thought Little Bear's porridge was *tasty*.

They are *quiet* so that the baby can sleep.

Tracie made a pouty face
after she ate the *sour* candy.

The clean clothes smell really *fresh*.

Pretty is how someone *looks*.

Spicy is how something *tastes*.

Soft is how something *feels*.

Musty is how something **smells**.

Loud is how something *sounds*.

I look

I taste

with my eyes

I feel

with my tongue

I have feelings

with my hand

I smell

Happy   Sad

I hear sound

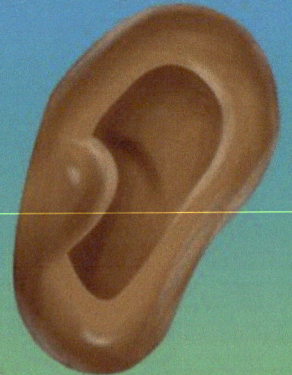

with my nose   Mad   Scared

with my ear

Can you make sentences about how people, places, and things look, taste, feel, smell and sound?

ABOUT OUR LEARNING SYSTEM

BLOOMING READERS

Blooming readers is not just a random series of books. It is a unique Early Reading Tool that simultaneously introduces strategically selected high frequency words, and parts of speech.

Try playing sentence games by putting nouns, verbs, and adjectives together taught in our books. When books are purchased in order, our sight words can be combined to form hundreds of sentences.

MORE TO LEARN

Using The Book

Read this book with your early reader. Touch the words in bold as you read them. Ask your child to show you the character in the book that the word is referring to.

Make it fun and relatable. Ask questions as you read to your child. "What do you think about_?" or "Would you like __?" "Does your sister __?" or "Have you ever __?"

Reading Ready - When your child is ready, allow him/her to read to you. Starting out, alternate the pages. You may read all the pages on the left and he/she read the pages on the right.

Beyond The Book

To give your child more practice with the sight words introduced in this book, try making flash cards.

What you'll need-All you need is a black marker and blank index cards or sentence strips.

How to use- If your goal is to teach your child the words in this book, read the book at least twice a week with your child. Also, review the sight word flash cards with your child at least three times a week for about five minutes.

Something to Consider-No need for a picture. Letters are, in a sense pictures. Often times when children use illustrated flash cards they are looking at the picture and not the word. The picture becomes a distraction for some children.

WORD LIST

fresh	spicy	smells	lovely
sick	cute	slow	short
big	dirty	hot	smelly
nice	cold	chubby	surprised
happy	mean	ugly	sweet
old	slim	sad	pretty
angry	clean	quiet	slow	shy
tasty	feels	sounds	sour	fast

VISUAL OF HOW TO USE THE INDEX CARDS WITH THE WORDS FROM THIS SERIES

| My | sister | is | messy | . |

| He | had | a | party | . |

| Do | you | like | cake | ? |

FOLLOW THE AUTHOR.

www.ingramcontent.com/pod-product-compliance
Lightning Source LLC
LaVergne TN
LVHW072054070426

835508LV00002B/98